# SURF DOG MIRACLES

## by Meish Goldish

**Consultant: Michael Uy**
**Owner of Surf Dog Abbie Girl**

PUBLISHING

New York, New York

## Credits

Cover and Title Page, © Nate Jones/PacificCoastNews/Newscom; Cover TR, © Lionel Hahn/AbacaUsa/Newscom; Cover CR, © AP Photo/Denis Poroy; Cover BR, © Lionel Hahn/AbacaUsa/Newscom; TOC, Mike Blake/Reuters/Newscom, 4, © Clint Brewer/Splash News/Newscom; 5, © Lionel Hahn/AbacaUsa/Newscom; 6, © Cindy Yamanaka/The Orange County Register/ZUMA Press/Newscom; 7, © Headlinephoto/Splash News/Newscom; 8, © FPG/Getty Images; 9, © AP Photo/Denis Poroy; 10, © Mike Blake/Reuters/Landov; 11L, © Lionel Hahn/AbacaUsa/Newscom; 11R, © Michael Uy; 12, © Nate Jones/PacificCoastNews/Newscom; 13, © Mike Blake/Reuters/Newscom; 14, © Jeffery R. Werner/IncredibleFeatures.com; 15, © Jeffery R. Werner/IncredibleFeatures.com; 16, © Alan Zasi/IncredibleFeatures.com; 17, © Tamandra Michaels/IncredibleFeatures.com; 18, © pawmazing.com for Incredible Features; 19, © Jeffery R. Werner/IncredibleFeatures.com; 20, © Mike Blake/Reuters/Newscom; 21, © Charlie Neuman/San Diego Union-Tribune/Zuma Press/Newscom; 22, © AP Photo/Dale Porter / Killerimage.com/PRNewsFoto/Helen Woodward Animal Center; 23, © Michael Uy; 24, © Nate Jones/PacificCoastNews/Newscom; 25T, © Dale Porter/Killerimage.com; 25B, © Dale Porter/Killerimage.com; 26, © Nate Jones/PacificCoastNews/Newscom; 27, © Banks/Splash News/Newscom; 28, © Mike Blake/Reuters/Newscom; 29TL, © cynoclub/Shutterstock; 29TR, © Eric Isselée/Shutterstock; 29BL, © Eric Isselée/Shutterstock; 29BR, © Eric Isselée/Shutterstock.

Publisher: Kenn Goin
Editorial Director: Adam Siegel
Creative Director: Spencer Brinker
Design: Dawn Beard Creative
Photo Researcher: Picture Perfect Professionals, LLC

*Library of Congress Cataloging-in-Publication Data*

Goldish, Meish.
  Surf dog miracles / by Meish Goldish.
    p. cm. — (Dog heroes)
  Includes bibliographical references and index.
  ISBN 978-1-61772-577-7 (library binding) — ISBN 1-61772-577-3 (library binding)
  1. Service dogs—Juvenile literature. 2. Surfing—Juvenile literature. 3. Animals as aids for people with disabilities—Juvenile literature. I. Title.
  HV1569.6.G656 2013
  362.4'048—dc23

                    2012007079

For more information, write to Bearport Publishing Company, Inc., 45 West 21st Street, Suite 3B, New York, New York 10010. Printed in the United States of America.

10 9 8 7 6 5 4 3 2 1

# Table of Contents

# Ruff Riders

One morning in September 2011, a large crowd gathered at the **shore** in Huntington Beach, California. The people had come to watch dozens of surfers ride the rolling ocean waves. Unlike most surfers, however, these athletes weren't balancing themselves on two legs. They were using four. Why? These surfboard riders were dogs! They were part of the 2011 Surf City Surf Dog **competition**.

Dog surfers and their owners at the 2011 Surf City Surf Dog competition

The Surf City Surf Dog competition is a three-day event held each fall in Huntington Beach, California. The town is nicknamed "Surf City USA" for its many ocean waves that are perfect for surfing.

Dogs of all sizes and **breeds** took part in the contest to see which water-loving **canine** could ride the waves the longest. In one **heat** for extra-large dogs, Sir Hollywood, an English bulldog, made the first long ride of the day. Stanley, a Chesapeake Bay retriever, and Molly Godiva, a chocolate Labrador retriever, also tried to ride the waves. More than a thousand fans cheered the dogs on. In the end, Sir Hollywood was declared the winner of the heat.

Sir Hollywood rides a wave.

# Winning Points

The Surf City Surf Dog competition is one of several dog surfing contests held each year in Southern California. As many as 80 dogs have taken part in a competition. Their goal is to stay on the surfboard while riding a wave to shore. Judges award points to each dog based on the length of the ride, the height of the wave, and the surfing style or tricks done by the dog.

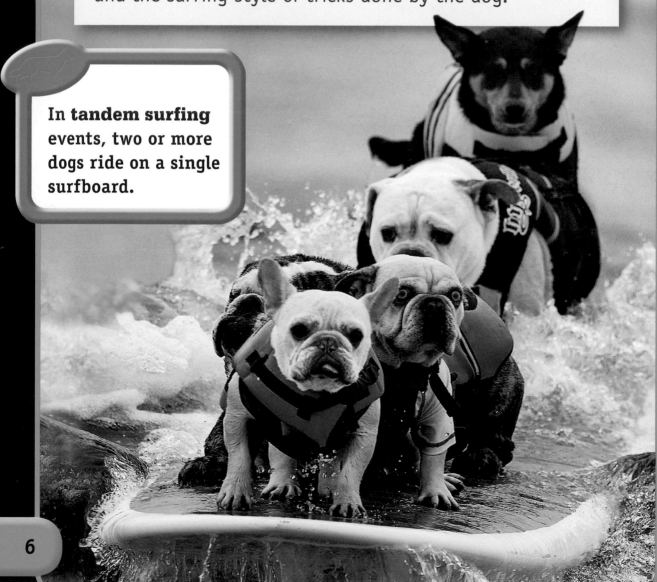

In **tandem surfing** events, two or more dogs ride on a single surfboard.

Extra points are given for more difficult rides. For example, dogs that stand on all four legs while surfing earn more points than those that sit or lie on the board. Also, recovering after almost falling off the board is worth more points than a calm, steady ride.

Surfing backwards and spinning around on a board are two tricks that people love to watch. This dog rode backwards for extra points.

# Early Surfing

Surf dog competitions are a fairly new kind of event. The very first contest, organized by the Loews Coronado Bay Resort in San Diego, California, was held in 2006. However, canines were surfing for fun long before then. As early as the 1920s, dogs and their owners were riding surfboards off the shores of California and Hawaii.

**Surf dogs, such as this one from the 1940s, have been riding ocean waves for many years.**

Philip K. Auna and his terrier Night Hawk were featured in early surfing photographs and films. A 1930 short silent movie titled *On the Waves at Waikiki* shows the pair surfing together in Hawaii. After catching a wave, Night Hawk was able to "hang ten" by gripping his front paws over the front of the wooden surfboard.

Like Night Hawk, Zoey grips the tip of the surfboard with her eight front toes.

When surfers "hang ten," they stand at the front of the surfboard and wrap all ten toes over the edge. Falling off the board and landing in the water is called a **wipeout**.

# Riding Alone

As surf dogs gained more skill on a surfboard, owners wanted to see if their canines could ride by themselves. The earliest known dog to surf **solo** was Rocky. He started showing off his amazing talent in the 1980s.

The best surfboard for dogs is made of foam, because a dog can grip it easily with its claws.

Smaller dogs, such as this one, usually use a six-foot (1.8-m) surfboard. Larger dogs ride on one that is eight feet (2.4 m) long.

Rocky's owner, Robin Marien, was a surfer. One day Robin was taking his surfboard into the water. When Rocky jumped on top, Robin pulled the board out into the ocean and gave it a push. To Robin's surprise, Rocky rode his first wave all the way to shore. He proved that a dog could stay balanced on a board without human help. Soon, other owners had their dogs surfing solo as well.

**Rocky surfing solo**

**Rocky led the way to solo surfing by other dogs, such as this one.**

# Go with the Flow

Dog surfing is an exciting and challenging sport. However, only a small number of dogs are able to do it. Not all canines find it fun or easy to ride rolling waves on a narrow board. How do surf dog owners train their pets? Many start by playing with their dogs in the ocean. Over time, a dog gets used to swimming.

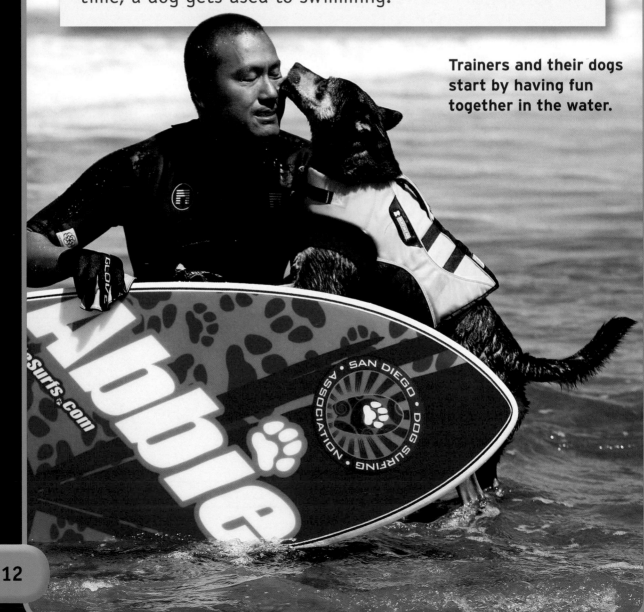

**Trainers and their dogs start by having fun together in the water.**

After a dog is comfortable in the water, its owner places the animal on a floating surfboard. The dog learns to balance itself by shifting its weight. Once the canine can easily stay balanced, the owner gently pushes the board into a small wave. If the dog enjoys the ride, its owner helps the furry surfer move on to larger waves.

Surf dog owners always stay close to their pets as they train them. The owner paddles out with the dog and swims back to shore with the animal. Owners must always be ready to rescue their dogs if they need help in the water.

# A Paw-fect Partner

One reason dogs surf is because it's fun for them. Ricochet, however, is a dog that goes one step further. She helps people with **disabilities** surf in the water with her. The golden retriever began in 2009, when her owner, Judy Fridono, introduced her to a teenage boy named Patrick Ivison.

Ricochet began learning how to surf when she was only eight weeks old.

**Ricochet and Patrick**

14

Patrick wasn't able to walk or stand because of a **spine** injury. He wanted to surf, but it was very difficult for him. Luckily, Ricochet was able to help. With Patrick lying down on the surfboard, Ricochet rode on the back. She **stabilized** the board by shifting her weight back and forth. Ricochet and Patrick were able to surf together—a true miracle.

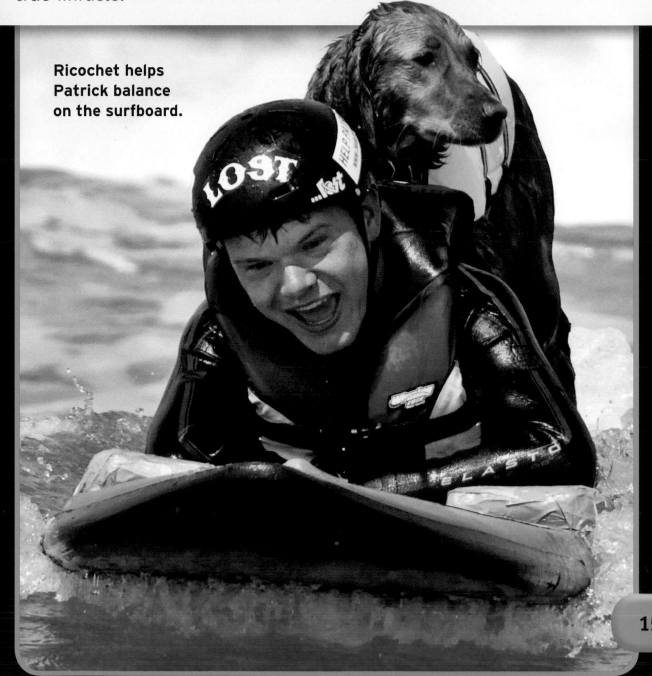

**Ricochet helps Patrick balance on the surfboard.**

# More Miracles

News of Ricochet's "miracle" ride with Patrick quickly spread. Soon, the golden retriever was helping other surfers who were disabled. She rode the waves with Sabine Becker, a woman who was born without arms. Sabine was amazed by the way Ricochet steadied the board. "Somehow, she does it so we're not off balance," Sabine said.

Ricochet was the first dog to surf with **special needs children** and people with disabilities.

Sabine Becker and Ricochet surfing together

Another surfing partner for Ricochet was Ian McFarland. He was a six-year-old boy whose brain had been damaged in a car accident. Before the injury, Ian had been learning to surf with his dad, but he was now afraid to go in the water. Ricochet changed that. After surfing with the dog, Ian was eager to return to the ocean—another miracle.

Ricochet helping Ian McFarland surf

# Money and Hope

Ricochet has raised the spirits of many surfers who are disabled. She's also raised money for them. For example, through Ricochet's **fund-raising** efforts, people have **donated** more than $7,000 to help pay for Ian McFarland's **therapy**.

**Ricochet presents Ian (left) with a big check.**

10735

DATE 6/20/10

THE
OF Ian McFarland                      $7500.00

Seventy five hundred and 00/100 _____ DOLLARS

SURFice dog Ricochet

EMO_____
⑆123000123⑆456 007890 0⑈

Over the years, Ricochet has done even more good deeds. She has raised money for other surfers with disabilities. She has also encouraged people to donate money to more than 150 **charities** that help people and animals in need. By 2012, Ricochet's fund-raising totaled more than $150,000!

One of the many charities that Ricochet has helped support is the Morris Animal Foundation, which raises money to treat dogs with cancer.

**Ricochet with Patrick Ivison (left) and Ian McFarland (right)**

# A Group Effort

Ricochet isn't the only surf dog that raises money for charity. In 2011, around 80 dogs raised more than $100,000 by competing in the sixth annual Surf Dog Surf-A-Thon in Del Mar, California. Of all the canine surfers, Buddy, a Jack Russell terrier, received the most points from judges. He earned the title "Best in Surf." It was the fifth time he had won the contest.

**Buddy riding a wave**

The money raised at the Surf Dog Surf-A-Thon went to the Helen Woodward Animal Center in Rancho Santa Fe, California. This organization provides many services, including taking care of homeless animals, running a hospital for horses, and delivering pet food to animal owners who are too old or weak to leave their homes.

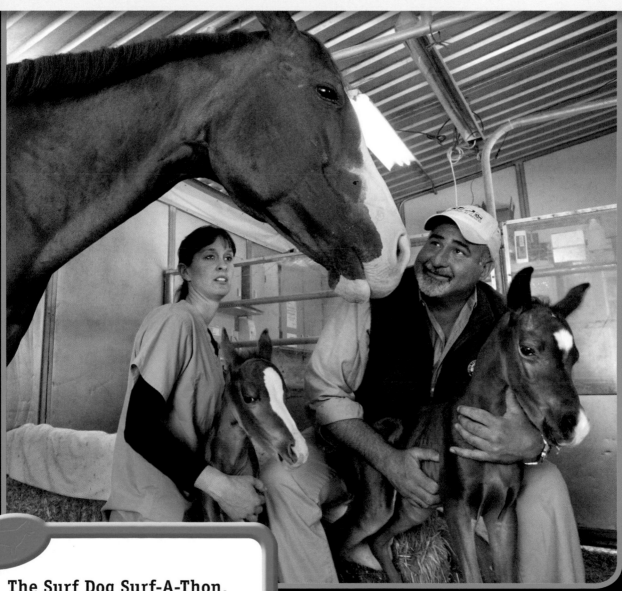

The Surf Dog Surf-A-Thon, run by the Helen Woodward Animal Center, is one of the largest surf dog competitions in the United States.

These twin baby horses, Angel and Sunny, were born at the Helen Woodward Animal Center's hospital for horses.

# Join the Club

Dog surfing has grown very popular over the years. Besides annual competitions, there are also surf dog organizations. One club is the So Cal Surf Dogs, based in San Diego. Several times during the summer, members meet at beaches to **socialize**, surf with their dogs, and enter contests together.

In addition, the club runs a Web site that offers advice on how to train a dog to surf. The site also shares tips for keeping surf dogs safe in the water. For example, owners are urged to have each dog wear a canine **flotation device**. It prevents dogs from drowning if they fall off the surfboard.

To stay safe, each of these dogs wears a flotation device.

The earliest surf dog organization, the San Diego Dog Surfing Association, began in 2008. It was the first club to insist that all dogs wear flotation devices and use soft boards—surfboards that are softer and safer than traditional boards made out of **fiberglass**.

# The World's Best

Every year, surf dogs become more skilled. At the Surf Dog Surf-A-Thon in 2010, an Australian kelpie named Abbie Girl won the contest with a perfect score. In one amazing **feat**, she jumped from her surfboard to another dog's board after its rider fell off. Abbie Girl rode the second board all the way to shore. It was the first time a dog had ever surfed on two boards on a single wave.

Abbie Girl is a very popular surf dog with her own Facebook page.

At the 2011 Surf City Surf Dog competition, Abbie Girl scored another dog-surfing first that soon became an official world record. She rode the longest wave ever surfed by a dog in **open water**. She traveled 65 yards (59 m)—more than half the length of a football field!

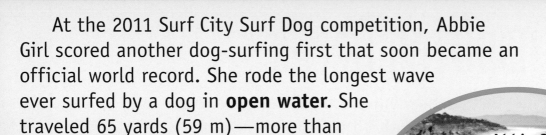

Abbie Girl with her Guinness World Records award

**GPS**

Abbie Girl's 2011 surfing record results were recorded by a **GPS** attached to her back. The record was the first ever awarded to a surf dog by Guinness World Records.

**The GPS on Abbie Girl's back measured the distance traveled by Abbie Girl in the water.**

# Inspiring Deeds

Abbie Girl's achievements are remarkable, especially considering her difficult start in life. Her owner, Michael Uy, had rescued her from a dog **shelter**. At first, Abbie was very shy and easily startled. Michael used swimming, surfing, and other sports as ways to help the canine become more outgoing and active. Today, Abbie **inspires** dog owners by showing them how much fun it can be to have an athletic dog.

Michael was able to help Abbie become a happier dog by teaching her how to surf.

Michael also uses Abbie's success story to help raise awareness for animal shelters. Her achievements show people how rescue dogs can go on to do amazing things.

Other surf dogs also continue to perform miracles both in and out of the water. For example, Ricochet still partners with surfers who are disabled. In addition, each year, surf dogs raise more and more money for people and animals in need. In the future, these amazing canines will surely keep riding the waves to success!

Because of her outstanding skills on the surfboard, Abbie Girl has been featured on Animal Planet and many television shows, as well as appearing in TV commercials and in newspapers.

# Just the Facts

- The Surf City Surf Dog competition includes more than just surfing events. Dogs can also take part in a fashion show and a costume contest, as well as a competition to see which canines look most like their owners.

- In 2010, Abbie Girl and several other surf dogs appeared in the movie *Marmaduke*.

- The So Cal Surf Dogs Web site (www.socalsurfdogs.com) includes information about more than 20 different surf dogs, including their favorite foods, toys, and activities.

- Any type of dog can become a surf dog, regardless of its breed or size. All that matters is its ability to ride ocean waves.

- Not all dogs wish to keep on surfing after trying it the first time. Owners should never force their dog to surf if the animal clearly does not like it.

- When Apple founder Steve Jobs introduced the iPad in 2010, he showed the video "Wet and Woofy," which featured the champion surf dog Buddy.

**Buddy riding a wave**

Golden retriever

Jack Russell terrier

Labrador retriever

English bulldog

**breeds** (BREEDZ) particular kinds of dogs

**canine** (KAY-nine) a member of the dog family

**charities** (CHA-ruh-teez) organizations that raise money to help people or animals in need

**competition** (*kom*-puh-TISH-uhn) a contest

**disabilities** (*diss*-uh-BIL-uh-teez) conditions that make it hard for a person to do everyday things such as walking, seeing, or hearing

**donated** (DOH-*nayt*-id) gave in order to help a charity or other group

**feat** (FEET) an achievement that shows great courage, strength, or skill

**fiberglass** (FYE-bur-*glass*) a strong material made from very fine threads of glass

**flotation device** (floh-TAY-shuhn di-VYESS) an item that a person or animal wears in order to float in the water; a life jacket

**fund-raising** (FUHND-*ray*-zing) collecting money for a cause

**GPS** (jee-pee-ESS) letters standing for Global Positioning System; a space-based navigation satellite system that provides accurate location information

**heat** (HEET) a round in a contest

**inspires** (in-SPYE-urz) encourages others to do things

**open water** (OH-puhn WAW-tur) water in an ocean or large lake that is not near shore

**shelter** (SHEL-tur) a place where homeless animals can stay

**shore** (SHOR) the land along the edge of an ocean, river, or lake

**socialize** (SOH-shuh-lize) to get together with people in order to talk and have a good time

**solo** (SOH-loh) when something is done by one person or animal

**special needs children** (SPESH-uhl NEEDS CHIL-druhn) children who have learning disabilities or have a hard time dealing with their emotions

**spine** (SPINE) the part of the skeleton that runs down the center of the back and helps people and some animals walk and move

**stabilized** (STAY-buh-lyezd) kept steady

**tandem surfing** (TAN-duhm SURF-ing) having surfers arranged one behind the other on the same board

**therapy** (THER-uh-pee) a treatment for an illness, injury, or disability

**wipeout** (WIPE-out) when a surfer falls off a surfboard and lands in the water

## Bibliography

**Anderson, Allen and Linda.** *Animals and the Kids Who Love Them: Extraordinary True Stories of Hope, Healing, and Compassion.* Novato, CA: New World Library (2011).

**Davis, Marcie, and Melissa Bunnell.** *Working Like Dogs: The Service Dog Guidebook.* Crawford, CO: Alpine Publications (2007).

**Warshaw, Matt.** *The Encyclopedia of Surfing.* Orlando, FL: Harcourt (2005).

## Read More

**Crump, A. K., ed.** *The Dog's Guide to Surfing: Hanging Ten with Man's Best Friend.* San Francisco, CA: TCB-Café Publishing (2005).

**Fogle, Jean M.** *Salty Dogs.* Hoboken, NJ: Wiley Publishing (2007).

**Jmo, Steve, and Janeta Hevizi.** *The True Story of Bilbo: The Surf Lifeguard Dog.* Penryn, UK: Cornish Cove Publishing (2008).

## Learn More Online

Visit these Web sites to learn more about surf dogs:

**www.abbiesurfs.com**

**www.loewssurfdog.blogspot.com**

**www.socalsurfdogs.com**

**www.surfcitysurfdog.com**

**www.surfdogricochet.com**

## Index

## About the Author

Meish Goldish has written more than 200 books for children. His book *Heart-Stopping Roller Coasters* was a Children's Choices Selection in 2011. He lives in Brooklyn, New York.